Irene Ayo Asuen

Destiny's Voices

Poetry, Vol. 1

QuietlySpeaking™

EMOTIONS

My character is defined.
I am more than one person
but never at the same time.
I am one or the other,
depending on the circumstances.
I react in the appropriate manner to all concerned.
Sometimes positive and sometimes negative.
And sometimes in manners that
I do not fully understand.
You see I am defined by my emotions.

I am human, I feel.
Occasionally, I am sad.
Sometimes it's so overwhelming, I cry.
Occasionally, I am happy.
Sometimes, it is so great that I am overjoyed.

And then I love.
Sometimes, so much so,
I am described as passionate.
At other times, I am confused, frustrated, lost,
and even empty inside but never emotionless.
Not even when I am expressionless.
You see, my feelings are controlled by my emotions.

I have a voice. I speak.
Depending on my position,
I am sometimes described as emotional.
I am soft-spoken, rude, aggressive, polite, nice, calm,
strong or sweet.
But I cannot help that about me.

My emotions can often be very overpowering.

I am human, I feel. I have a voice. I speak.
My character is defined by my emotions.
My emotions are overpowering.
My emotions build me.
My emotions make me the person that I am today.

DESIRE

I think of you and flames of desire
flare up in my heart.
My heartbeat becomes faster, and
there's certain softness within the depth of my soul.
Unconsciously, I smile as I breathe
in anticipation of what
I expect to feel when I see you.

My heart speaks a simple language.
It is the language of desire. I want you.
Not for a moment and not just for tomorrow
but for always.
Because in my heart burns an eternal flame.
It is the flame of desire.

You are my desire.
My heart understands this and my
soul knows for certain.
It is a strong feeling and a passionate
sensation that runs
through my being when I think of you.
I didn't plan this. It simply happened
when I met you.
I felt desire.

STRANGER

Each morning, same time, he enters the train
and immediately takes a seat.
He buries his head in his paper,
oblivious to his environment,
and quite unaware that she is admiring him.
She wonders what his name is.

She does not see a wedding band.
Quite naturally, she assumes that he is not married.
The thought crosses her mind that he might be gay.
Otherwise he probably has some
special girl in his life.
She hopes not.

She wonders if he notices her at all. She hopes so.
She wants to speak to him but has
yet to muster enough courage.
She has never been in this type of situation before.
A total stranger is the object of her admiration.

What to do? How to approach him?
She is terrified of rejection.
What a dilemma.
She knows absolutely nothing about him.
After all, he is a stranger.
Her stranger.

She thinks about him a lot and looks forward
to seeing him each day on the train
though unbeknown to him.
He is the object of her fancy,

and the reason for her glow.

She just wishes she has the courage to
say something to him. Maybe one day.
For now, he is still a stranger...her stranger

REFLECTIONS

The unknown is the reason for my fear,
and my worries are the burdens that wear me down.
Inspiration from above, and everyday experience
give me hope.

Hope is the reason for my courage,
and my courage is the source of my strength
on my quest for a better tomorrow.

Each step in life has a rough surface
that takes me to a piece of my future.
The future is a part of my life that I can't
change once that stage is over.
Because yesterdays are forever gone.

So I tread each step very carefully,
with a little prayer and a little hope
that the next step in life I take,
will be smoother than the last,
and the next stage in my life will be
better than the last.

I CLOSE MY EYES

I close my eyes and I see you.
As I watch you coming toward me,
Your steps are slow and deliberate.
Your expression is intense with desire.
I feel warm inside as I wait for you.
Your eyes focus on me.
Just me.

I close my eyes and I feel you.
Your touch is tender but the effect is electric.
I have never felt so right.
I feel strange yet I feel safe.
It is something about you.
As though you and I are supposed to happen.
Just us.

I close my eyes and I taste you.
You are warm and sweet and salty and safe.
We just fit.
I feel completely at ease because it feels so right.
You make me feel whole.
You are a part of my being.

I close my eyes and I know your face
You are the face of my heart.
I feel you in being, my mind and my soul.

I close my eyes and I hear your voice.
I am so in tuned to you.
You are the sound of my heartbeat.

I close my eyes and I know your walk.
I meet you every time I close my eyes
I close my eyes and I know you.
I feel you completely.
I just know your person.
You are the other half of me.
You are love.

MY INNER VOICE

I need to know that I count.
I need to know that I make a difference in the world.
It will make me feel that there is a purpose for my
place in the world.

I need to know that in my absence
I will be missed, if only for a short while.
It will make me feel important
as well as appreciated.

I need to know that I am loved totally,
completely and unconditionally.
It will make me feel as though I belong,
and life is worth living.

I need to know that I will not be
laughed at for any reason.
It will give me the courage I need to take risks.

I need to know that I will be safe wherever I go.
This way I know I will be back home safe.

However, life is unpredictable and
the world is not a kind place.
So no matter how much I need to now,
like everyone else, I can only hope.

RESTLESS

I look up to the skies for answers to my problems.
I don't hear any and I don't see any signs
that there will be reason to smile soon.

I go back to on my bed in sadness,
and curl up in a fetus position, trying in vain
to shield myself from the troubles looming over me.

I try to go to sleep but not to much avail.
I am too restless and fitful to get a good night's sleep.
My mind is too crowded
with worries to do much else.

Finally, unable to bear it any longer,
I get up from my bed.
Looking like hell and with tears in my eyes,
I go out into the night and scream my lungs out,
hoping for some answers.

Tired and exhausted from screaming and crying,
I go back inside and once again, lie down on my bed
in a fetus position.
Strangely enough, I felt much calmer
and managed to drift off to sleep.

I know things are going to be better in the morning.

DESTINY'S VOICES

In the quiet of the morning before the dawn of day
as I take my morning walks,
I speak silently, I listen quietly.
I hear myself, I think and I smile. I have a voice.
I have an audience. I am my audience,
and so are other early risers,
the whistling birds, the chirping squirrels,
the crawling ants, the gentle breeze and the rest of
nature. We are my audience.
We are one. We are each other's stories.

Who am I? Well, I am everything you imagined
and nothing you expected.
I believe we learn the best life lessons from the most
unexpected things, people and places.
We meet each other all the time, everyday.
We are visible but also invisible.
We see each other and yet we don't.
But we just know.
because we are all pieces of each other's destinies.
We are each other's stories.
We are destiny's voices.

They say actions speak louder than words,
but actions are words…silent words.
We read them in books.
We speak and read poetry. We drink them in mugs.
We express them on plaques.
We say them with our gestures.
We say them from our hearts.

We cry them in comfort, relief, pain and happiness.
We use them as vehicles for self-expression.
They give life to our personalities.

Words are powerful. Words give us hope.
Words are our natural-born tools.
Words make us feel free when we express them.
I feel free with words. I am heard.
I am visible. I belong.
I have an audience in everything,
everywhere, and everyone.

As the day fades into the night,
I feel my audience deem and my voice diminish.
Yet, I still want to speak.
Words give me life. I still have a voice.
Hear me, read me, and think me
as I speak in many ways.
Take a minute to pause as I
hope you listen quietly while
I speak silently in my destiny's voice.

.

PROMISE

I promise to care about you
if you promise to care about me.
I promise to lend you my shoulder in case
you should ever need one.

I promise to hope for you if you promise
to hope for me too.
I promise to dream for you if you
promise to dream for me.

I promise to be your friend forever,
in good times and bad times,
if you promise to be my friend in good times
and bad times too.

I promise to love you unconditionally,
if you promise to love me unconditionally.

For friendship sake, for love's sake
and for peace sake,
I simply promise never ever to quit on you,
if you promise never ever to quit on me too.

WINGS

I am down but not out.
It may seem that I am sinking
and the pit may seem bottomless.
Yet I know the pit is not as deep as it looks.
Otherwise, there are hooks on the sides
from which I shall soon climb out with.

Once out, as I know I surely will,
I will soar to great heights,
and fly like a bird with my wings fully spread,
because I know I will be free.

Yes, I will indeed be free!
Free of pain and hurt, and distrust and hatred.
Free of skepticism and doubt,
and failure and disappointment.
But most of all, I will be free to be me.

Yes, I will be free!
Free to express my ideas and to think I can,
and will be the best.
And to put me first, once in a while.
Free to pursue my dreams and goals,
and to believe in myself.
Free to think I am beautiful on the inside
as well as on the outside.
Yes, I will be free!

Free to overcome obstacles no matter how big.
Free to believe that I deserve the best out of life.
I will indeed be free to love, hope,

and to have faith in the world.

My wings will be spread wide, strong, and majestic.
Just ready to take the world by storm.
I will surely rise and soar to great heights.
Because I know I will indeed be free.

YOU MATTER

We met when we were very young.
Little did I know we are supposed
to be friends for life.
Though life threw us a curve ball,
it happened exactly the way it was supposed to.

I know I sometimes come out as rough on the edges,
and I don't often say how much
you mean to me as a friend
but you do matter to me. A lot.
I do appreciate you and I thank God,
you are my friend.

We went our separate ways according to God's design.
But it is almost as if we were still
in each other's shadows
all those years we were each doing our thing.
Because just when I needed you the most,
you reappeared like God's angel to me.
And we fell right into place just like old times.

So I say, thank you for encouraging me to go on
and reminding me that I can count on you
when I feel hopeless.
Thank you for being my sounding board
when I needed to vent.
Thank you for making me feel visible
when I feel invisible.
Thank you for being a safety net for me
when I feel like I am falling.
Thank you for tolerating my sometimes-harsh words
even when they are sometimes misdirected.

Know that I do appreciate you.

Most of all, thank you for accepting me
for me just the way I am.

From me to you, you'll always have a friend in me.
I promise to always be your friend without question,
without judgment, and with complete honesty.
No matter what happens, I promise never,
ever to quit on you.
You matter that much.

LOST LOVE

I'm hurt, I'm sad and I'm weeping.
I can no longer be the same because
I'm no longer whole.
A part of me is gone, gone forever
with your absence,
my love, my lost love.

Gone are the days of fighting,
and the joys of making up.
Gone are the days of enjoying
the pleasures of life together.
Gone are the days of helping each
other through life's challenges.
Gone forever are the days of eating,
sleeping, and waking up together.
Gone forever is my treasured love.

I am confused now.
Where do I go from here?
How do I go on by my lonesome?
How do I fill the void in my life now? I simply can't.
It's much too difficult to continue without you,
my love, my lost love.
You are all I ever need and all I ever wanted.
I was happy.

I was content with the love we shared.
I was blissful. I truly believed in life.
Now my light has gone off.
Life is hard to live without you.

My one true shot at happiness is gone.
Gone forever with you, my love, my lost love.

FRIENDS

Over the years we have come to understand each
other as people, and love each other as friends.
We have come to understand each other's feelings,
and respect each other's views and opinions.
Yet never loose sight of our friendship.

We have been able to openly express our pains
and our happiness, our dreams and our thoughts.
All without fear of rejection
and judgment from each other.
We have come this far through
life's difficult steps by
encouraging each other not to give up hope
for a better tomorrow.

We have cried and we have laughed.
And we did them together.
We have been angry at each other for periods of time
but in the end we still came out as friends.
I know without a shadow of doubt that
even if the world turned against us,
we will still be friends by the end of time.

So even when our losses seem overwhelming
and life deals us a cruel blow,
at least we will know that our friendship
was the best thing that
could ever happen to us in our lifetime.

A friendship that is as solid as a mountain rock
and as powerful and unshakable as
our faith in each other.

Most of all, a friendship that is as strong as our
determination to see it through
till the end of our time.

.

AS FRIENDS AND AS LOVERS

You are my better half.
When I feel depressed and sure I can't go on,
you are there to keep me strong and encourage me.

You are my glorious half.
When I feel joyful and need to
share my victorious moments,
you are there to share it with me
to make me feel even happier.

You are my solid half.
You are there to listen to me even
when I sound silly.
You understand me even
when I can't explain myself.
You are always there to make me
feel good about myself.

Indeed, you are my very best friend.
I am sure we were destined to be together.
It must have been written in the stars by
a higher Being, even before we were created.

So I say thank you for being my friend,
but most of all,
I thank God for bringing you into my life
and connecting us so perfectly together.

DESTINY'S LOVE

I knew it was you when I first saw you.
I don't know how, but I just knew.
There was just something about you.
Still can't place my finger on it
but the connection was there, and I just knew.

You declared that you wanted me.
You declared that you loved me
after a mere two weeks without having met me in
person…and I believed!
Me, the skeptic. Me, the cynic. Yet, I believed.
I believed because I felt the exact same thing.

I knew it was you when I felt my heart race and my
body tingle at the mere sound of your voice.
I knew when I got on a plane on a whim to a place
I had never been to before, just to meet you for the
very first time. That's when I knew.
I am usually quite rational, quite logical, even with
matters of the heart.
Love breeds courage I guess.

I knew when I met you for the very first time,
and I felt like jumping your bones right there and then.
I just knew it was you.
Thank goodness, you felt the same way.

I knew it was you when your kiss made my feet
curl and my stomach flutter.
I knew it was you when for the first time in my life,
I actually imagined having a love child

with someone called you.

I knew when a friend asked how I felt about you,
and without hesitation or a single doubt,
I declared that you are the only one that
I have ever been willing to make a fool of myself for.
She understood what that meant.
That's when I knew for sure that it was you.

I knew that I was in too deep when you flipped
the script on me and surprised me by your personality.
You are a man in every sense of the word,
confident in your emotions for me, your demand for
me and your declaration that you and I were each other's
loves designed by destiny. It just was.
That's when I knew.

I was floored by the strength of your person and the
power of my emotions for you too.
That's not how it usually works.
I usually guard my heart fiercely and control who
gets a piece.
Yet, you came from nowhere and took all of it boldly,
unexpectedly, without warning, and without permission.
That's when I knew it was you.

And then sadly, I didn't know what to do with
my emotions. It was all too much.
My feelings for you overwhelmed me.
So I did what I do best when it
comes to matters of the heart:
I turned tail and ran.

But that led to an unexpected problem.
I hurt me too.
You were still under my skin.
Yet, you refused to leave my heart.

In everyone else that I met, you were
there in their faces.
I couldn't see them because all I saw was you,
all day and in every person. And when
I went to sleep at night,
you were right there in my dreams too.

You were also in my words when I spoke and
in my memories of our times together.
All the time we were apart, you were always there,
consuming my heart, occupying my thoughts.
That's when I knew that I made a mistake.
I should never have let you go.
Because it was you, all along.

I knew when during our years apart,
I thought of you every single day.
Finally, after an overwhelming sense of unable to
bear it any longer and wondering about you,
I took a chance and reached out to you;
hoping your heart still belonged to me.

I knew it would be okay when you said you still
had feelings for me, and then you declared that
you wanted to have a love child with me.
That's when I knew my feelings were true and
destiny does not lie.

When we reconnected, I knew it was still you
when you echoed every thought that I had had
about us when we were apart.
I knew the minute you declared that you missed me,
that it was going to be alright again.
I knew it was you when you told me you wanted
me back, and I replied that I wanted you back too.
That's when I was assured it was you.

I don't even recognize myself. This is so not me.
My head thinks about you all the time.
My heart aches for you all the time.
My body craves you all the time.
I am so glad our time apart did not break us.
We have reconnected without missing a beat.
We were one heart then, and still one heart now.
We are still us. We are still one
That's when I knew it was you.

You keep me guessing. You keep me challenged.
You make me vulnerable.
You make me willing to take risks.
You make me confused. You keep me certain.
You simply make me happy.
I just know that it was meant to be you.

You are nothing I expected, and everything
that I have always wanted.
Everyone said that I would know when I met you.
They were right. I just knew the moment we met
many years ago that it was you.
It has always been you. It will always be you.

Destiny gave me you. Destiny gave you me.
Destiny gave us each other.
You knew it was me and I knew it was you.
You are my Destiny's Love.

GONE
(Osarugue)

I remember the exact moment I was told.
I remember how I felt.
I could not breathe. My heart felt like it was squeezing.
The pain was intense. I closed my eyes shut.
I hoped it was a bad dream.

I remember the last time I last saw you
but I never dreamt it would really be the last time.
The memories of us: sisters.
How painful, how bittersweet, how sad.
How short our time on earth together was. So not fair.
The pain still so raw as though you left yesterday.

There is no closure.
It doesn't get better over time. It just is.
I always remember you my sister.
I always live you.
Everyday, each year, I remember you.
I can never forget you. I don't want to.

You live everyday in my heart.
My heart bleeds when I think of you.
Yet I am thankful to have known you.
I celebrate your birthday every year.
I feel you looking down on me.
I say your name quietly.

We are still six, not five. United by blood.
I remember how beautiful it felt

to have you as a younger sister.
I remember you always, my sister.
I feel your light shinning down.
I say your name softly.
I see your smile in my mind.
It feels so real.
Osarugue, I remember you with so much love.

QUIETLY SPEAKING, SILENTLY LISTENING

I am screaming silently at the top of my voice.
I am speaking to you but you are not hearing me.
Please turn around and speak to me.
Hear my heart and hear my voice.
You are deaf to my voice yet I am silently speaking.
Read my face and you'll know.

Your person intrigues me.
Look at me. My expression is openly inviting.
I am drawn to you but you don't notice.
There's a sense of mystery about you.
Yet you are unaware of your mystique.

I have an idea; let's say hello.
Let's say something to each other.
Let us speak.
It's the first step toward getting to know each other.
It's the first step toward what could be.

Just one thing; I am the only one speaking.
You do not hear me as I silently speak,
and quietly hope to hear the sound of your voice.

My lips may not be moving, but my heart is screaming.
These are the voices of my head.
These are the sounds of my mind.
Give me something to go by. Tell me you hear me.
Tell me you notice.
You intrigue me. I am drawn to your heart.

Feel my heart beat as I quietly wait
for you to hear me.
I speak silently but it is written on my face.
I wait hopefully as I quietly listen
to the sound of your heart.

THREE STAGES, THREE NEEDS

Love me now when I am young and
helpless and still a baby.
I can't walk and I can't speak because I am still too
young to do these things.
But the smile on my face and the joy in my eyes will
express my content.
And I will remember this love as I grow up.

Love me now when I am a teenager
and still growing.
I am confused and not sure who I am
or what I want to be.
I do not quite have a sense of direction but
I will know there is someone
who cares enough to guide me.
And I will remember this love as I grow older.

Love me now when I am old and helpless again.
I have been through life's tough challenges
and made it to old age.
But my body is worn and I ache all over.
I can't walk without a cane and I am not
as strong as I once was.

My sight is weak, my body is slow and my
days are numbered.
Love me now, as I grow older.

For when I am gone, I will remember you

in my new world as you feel my love through
the three stages of your own life.

All I ask is that you love me now as
I go through my own three stages.

DESTINY

The stirring in my heart, the boredom,
the pull, the restlessness.
Tugging and pulling, it is time to seek again.
Where to go? What to do?
Not sure. Still seeking.
I'll tell you when I get there.
I'll tell you when I know.

Anxiously waiting. Anticipating. Excited.
The unknown. Destiny waits.
In a face, in an object moment, in an instance.
All at once everything changes.
And my course is forever altered.
No need to plan, no need to figure.
It just is.

The pull, the stirrings in my heart, the restlessness.
Unforeseen but dragging me through
a predetermined path, to a predetermined
point by a force unknown.

When will I stop?
I'll know when I get there.
I'll know because everything stops,
and there is nothing but calmness.
There is peace. I am finally home.
I am finally in tune with Destiny.

HIS EYES

It is all in his eyes.
His eyes speak volumes,
telling a thousand contrasting stories.
Sad, happy, contented, afraid, proud.
Impossible to translate yet
pleading to be understood.
Drawing me closer, yet pushing me away.
His eyes bring an aura of mystery to his person.

It is all in his eyes.
They look like precious gems;
Constantly changing colors.
Drowning in twin pools.
Not giving much yet telling all.
His eyes are a force to be noticed.
They seduce without so much as a flicker.
His eye radiate an allure that cannot be denied.

His eyes dig into my soul, into my heart,
and into my being.
His eyes fill me with strength, with security,
and with courage to face the world.
His eyes are in a word: trusting.
They radiate an appeal, a confidence
that cannot be denied.

His eyes show conflicting emotions.
Strong yet vulnerable, proud yet humble,
sensitive yet indifferent.
Never betraying, never hinting
just how he would react in any given situation.

His eyes make me feel like I could not,
would never lie to him.

It is all in his eyes, the story of his person.
The history, present and future of his person.
The boy that he was, the guy that he is,
and the man that he still hope to become.
One glance was all it took to draw me in.

DANCE

It was the moment. It was the time. It was the place.
Open dance floor under the starry skies.
Full moon smiling in approval.
It was the time for romance.
The music was beautiful.
They were all in their elements.
Everyone, including him and her.

Two strangers, spell-bounded by each other.
They spotted each other from opposite sides of
the floor at the same exact moment.
He, a tall handsome stranger.
She, a beautiful damsel in a stunning gown.

As though on cue, everyone
on the dance floor moved
aside as they made their way slowly
but deliberately toward each other.
As though a powerful force was
drawing them toward other.
Their eyes never leaving each other.
No second was to be wasted.

When they finally met up, they did not speak.
Words were not needed.
He simply took her in his arms and
they dance for the moment,
lost in each other's worlds.

The connection was real without questions,
without a doubt.

It was a magical moment.
It was their dance.

DESTINY'S ANGUISH

What about us? What about love?
What happened to us?
What about our promises to each other?
Why did we break-up? Or did we?
The pull, the anguish, the pain, the regret.

Are we the ones that got away from each other?
Do we stand a second chance?
Are we too scared to try again?
Or are we willing to fight away the obstacles?
We almost had, we almost were,
and perhaps we still can.
Oh, the anguish.

We tried for a while to stay away from each other.
And it worked for a while. I was doing just fine.
And then from nowhere,
the memories came flooding back.
And the dreams now come frequently.
The dreams of you, of our memories together, our joy.
Oh what anguish!

We reached out again to each other
and the feelings were still the same.
Just as if time never past.
Just as if nothing ever separated us.
Just as if we were still us, living in the connected
moment, time standing still.
Just living in us, with us, for us. Just you and I.
The pull, the memories, the expectations, the hope.
Perhaps still to be.

Perhaps never to be again.
Oh what anguish!

You are still here. I am still here.
We almost were. Same thoughts. Not a coincidence.
You stole something from me.
You never gave it back to me. You stole my heart.
The pull, oh the pull. How agonizing.
You hold me captive. You won't let go.
It hurts. I'm in limbo. Stop pulling me in.
The pull is so strong. It's hard to fight back.
Oh what anguish!

We've got to stop running.
We've got to come back to one.
We've just got to stop the anguish.
It's time to get back to one.
Or maybe we were the ones that got
away from each other.
Perhaps we'll never know.
Perhaps, we will always wonder.
Destiny's cruel faith on us.
Oh what anguish!

SONGS OF THE HEART

My heart sings a sad silent song,
and somehow you hear it.
My heart sings a silent joyful song and you hear it too.
My heart bleeds with silent pain.
And you reach out to comfort me because
you feel it too.

My heart cries silently for someone to share my
triumphs and happiness,
And the smile and pride on your face tell me you do.
Because your heart knows my heart only too well.
When we are apart, I feel what you feel
and I know you feel what I feel.

When we are standing just a short distance apart,
I know exactly what you think,
and you know exactly what I think.

Is it a mystery?
I thought so at first, but now I realize not.
because there's only one heart for every two people.
And you and I each have the two halves of one heart
that makes us breathe and feel as one.
One heart, which connects us with that special magic
that happens just between the two of us.

SKEPTIC

I was a believer for sure. I was a believer of life.
I believed in sisterhood and brotherhood.
I believed in sharing and giving.
I believed I could be safe anywhere, anytime.
Because I believed everyone had a loving heart.

I was also a believer of love.
I believe in romance and love at first sight.
I believe in the knight in shinning
armor whisking me off
on a white horse to romantic paradise.

I believe in red roses, candlelit dinners and soft music
playing in the background.
I also believed in holding hands and
walking in the parks.

And yes, I was a believed in family too.
You know, father, mother, brothers and sisters.
And of course the family pet.
I believed that daddy would always protect and
provide for his family,
and mommy could solve any problem.
I believed my brother would always look out for me,
and my sister and I could confide
in each other anytime.

Yes, I believed in family.
I believed we would always come together
at the end of the day
and have nice family dinners amid conversations and

banters of the day's activities and future plans.
I believed in family fun times and family standing
behind each other in times of crisis.
I believed in family saying
I love you each night before
going to sleep or after phone conversations.
I believed in family talking and staying together.

Of course I believed in friendship.
I believed that friends were forever
through thick and thin.
I believed in secrets between friends,
shoulders to cry on,
and friends never disappearing when
things got tough.
I believed that fair-weather friends never existed.
I believed in friends being there in good times
and bad times.
I believed friendships did not have seasons.
Yes, I was a believer with a doubt.

I was a believer of life but I was also a dreamer.
I believed in a fantasy world.
I believed so much, I lost sight of reality.
Not anymore. Reality jolted me from my fantasy.
I woke up from my slumber.
I stopped believing.

GOD'S PERFECT WORK

To him from her:
I needed a change so I took the courage to make the
first step to a new city. It was harder than I expected
but I know I took the exact step that was designed as
path of the course of my life by God.
I know this because I found you.
You are my precious gift from God.

You see through my toughness and
cut through to the heart of me.
You let yourself be when you are around me.
You don't just love me, you actually like me.
You accept me with all my imperfections.
Because of this, I feel all is well with the world.
Thank God for my gift of you.

To her from him:
I saw you, and I knew right away.
We were meant to be.
There is a light about you that brightens up my day.
I am secure in your presence.
You are my gift from God.
You accept me completely despite my imperfections.
You actually like being in my space.
You are the joy of my life.
I would not change a thing about you.
You are perfect for me because
you are part God's work.

For him and her:
God bless us both everyday.
We are are God's gifts to each other.
Lifting each other up, praying together
and loving together.

When we look into each other's eyes,
Let's always remember God does not make mistakes.
He brought us together in
the exact manner that he intended.
We are each other's perfection and reflections of
destiny's designs.
We are God's perfect work.

HURT

My heart won't stop hurting.
I feel this ache each time I think of you.
I think of you every single day,
no matter how hard I try not to.
It's been over a year now and I still can't forget you.
You are as real to me as the very first time we met.

You are my first true love. My only love.
I can't seem to let go of you, no matter what I do.
I still love you as passionately as I did
when we first connected.
I want you back completely and
totally till the end of time.
I know without a doubt, you at it for me.

I compare everyone else to you.
They are temporary. You are permanent.
You are my destiny.
You are the man I am supposed to love
completely for the rest of my life,
without condition, without hesitation
and with all I have to give.
Across time, across age, across distance
and across cultures,
I am yours and you are mine.

It's time we bridge the pieces of our hearts
because we are only barely existing.
We need each other to function.
I need you. I want you. I love you completely.

I am the one that usually does the running away.

Yet this time, you are the one I want to run to.
You are my heart. I am yours to love.
You are mine to love. Always, now and forever.
You are the only one that can heal my hurt.

MY HEART, MY LOVE, MY SOUL

Come back to me my love. My arms are wide open.
Your absence takes away a part of my soul.
I don't feel whole without you in my life.
I am trying to forget how painful it is,
not to be with you.

I am doing different things
and going to different places.
I am meeting different people, but still to no avail.
I feel your presence at every function, and see your
face in everyone.
My heart is completely shattered and the
pieces can only be glued back
with your special touch.

My love, my heart, my soul, stops the endless flow
of my tears and kiss away my sadness.
Please remove this loneliness
from the depth of my being,
and make me whole again. Come back to me.
I am completely helpless and
you are the only comfort I know.

My love, my heart, my soul, my arms are wide open,
just waiting to embrace your person.
Please come back and heal my wounded being,
so I can start living again.

REFLECTIONS

The unknown is the reason for my fear,
and my worries are the burdens that wear me down.
Inspiration from above, and everyday
experiences give me hope.

Hope is the reason for my courage,
and my courage is the source of my strength
on my quest for a better tomorrow.

Each step in life has a rough surface
that takes me to a piece of my future.
The future is a part of my life that I can't
change once that stage is over.
Because yesterdays are forever gone.

So I tread each step very carefully,
with a little prayer and a little hope,
that the next step in life I take,
will be smoother than the last, and the next stage in
my life will be better than the last.

IMPERFECT

His eyes light up whenever he sees me.
He is a simple kind of guy.
What I like best about him?
Him. All of him. His person.
He is simple and imperfect.
Yet, he is my perfect person.

His smile is genuine and infectious.
His heart is honest and sincere.
He makes many mistakes. He is flawed.
Some days, I don't even like him.
Yet I love him all the time, everyday.

His emotions are deep and real.
He is open about his insecurities.
He is not afraid to share his feelings.
Sometimes he is uncertain,
and he gets mad and frustrated.
But that's okay. He is human after all.
And his imperfections are also his qualities.
They make him uniquely him.

His gestures are also endearing.
Unexpectedly, he presents me with quirky gifts.
And every time, I squeal in delight at
his innocent display of affection.

We are not perfect together.
We have our ups and downs.
But in our hearts, we are in perfect sync.
We are each other's perfectly imperfect persons.
We just fit like answers to the puzzles of our lives.

What I like best about him?
Him. All of him. Just him.
Simple, human and not quite imperfect.

PRIME

I am at the prime of my life,
and peak of my time.
I am young, smart, beautiful, and confident.
I can make the best out of my life.
Because very simply, I am at the peak of my life.

I have a zest for life and I live it to the
fullest each day.
Why not? It is the right time to do so.
I make bold decisions and I take risks.
Because that is what living is all about.
Besides, I am at my prime.

If I stumble or fall or if I make the wrong choice,
I can always get up and try again.
Because at this time of my life,
my strength is at its best
and I am relentless in my determination.

I look forward to living each day.
I look forward to life's challenges.
I fight my battles as they come.
I win some and I loose some.
But in the end I am really a winner.
Because, whether I win or loose,
I learn a lesson from each battle.
And I use each experience for bigger and
better things that come my way.

Sometimes, I create my own opportunities
because I can't settle for less than the best.
After all, I am at my peak and should be enjoying life.

After a while, I would have past my prime,
and I will not be as fast or as sharp as I am now.
My confidence will be less and I will feel old.
But for now I am at the prime and peak of my time.
I don't want to have any regrets later.
Just fond memories and great stories.

THE HEART OF ME

I have never felt like this before.
It happened without warning.
I never thought I'd feel this way.
It's something I can't describe.

I felt I would be prepared,
yet it happened without warning.
You surfaced from nowhere.
You were not even in my radar.
I saw your picture and I immediately felt the flutter.
You were different. You are different
And yet I haven't actually met you.

I prayed for me to know you when I see you,
and for you to know me when you see me
I prayed, oh how I prayed that
it would happen to me.
I hoped and I imagined every scenario possible.

Yes, I have seen you in a vision and
I believed you were there somewhere.
Yet, at the same time, I felt it was impossible.
It could never happen to me.
Good things simply just don't happen to me

And then there you were; a distance away.
We both felt it. We connected across the ocean,
several miles from each other.
Like we had known each other forever.

Separated by the Black Sea and the Atlantic Ocean,

Never having actually met,
yet connecting by our hearts.
We've only had two conversations.
Yet we both feel like we found the missing
pieces of our hearts with each other.

I don't know why but I think about you all the time.
You invade my thoughts, you make my body tingle.
I feel warm each time I think of you.
You are in my heart. You are the face of my heart.

It's like you invited yourself to
my life without permission
and then you stole my heart just like that.
Funny, I don't want it back
because you said I stole yours too.
I think mine is safe with you.
And you should know yours is safe with me too.

Usually, I run from my feelings.
I run from intimacy. I run, and then I search,
wondering what it is that I am looking for.
But then you came along and I just knew
it was safe to stop running.

The best part is that you feel the same
way about me.
Together as we make our way through life,
we know are one.
We are each other's homes.

RACE

In the race of my life, in pursuit of my goals.
Once was close but fell and my race was broken.
So very close yet so far away. Told to start again.
Hard to start afresh in the beginning of the line.
Heard the gun go off but started a second slower.
Now I am counting on determination
to see me through.

Still I am in the race of my life like so many others.
The track seems endless and
there are other races that I have to run.
But first I need to finish this one so
I can start the next one.
Determination is what counts.

I see people racing for all they are worth.
And I see others slowing down.
I also see people dropping out of the race
and giving up on their lives' goals.
They are not trying hard enough.
Or maybe they are. Either way, I understand.

I see myself panting and puffing,
and thinking of giving up on the race too.
Yet a little voice deep down
inside me encourages me
in a gentle voice not to give up.
It tells me the finish line is too close
for me to quit now.

The red tape is just within inches of me.

There are also flowers, medals and a
golden trophy waiting for me.
The voice is nudging me on.
Nice to know someone still cares.

I need all the determination that
I can muster to take these last few steps.
The voice says not to give up because I am capable
of not just finishing the race but winning it too.
I must not let this voice down.
I must not disappoint myself.
I have to finish this race.

My prizes are waiting.
Just waiting for me to pick them up.

NIGHT'S BEAUTY

Peaceful as the moonlit night,
You take your place as night's beauty.
A picture of innocence, unaware of
life's harsh reality.
So perfect to watch you sleep as I drink up
your form with my eyes.
And forget if even for a short while,
my own worries.
If only, oh if only the night would last forever with
you lying by my side.
My night's perfect beauty.

MEMORIES

The memories are forever.
Our very own treasure.
The times at the beach; splashing, playing
and just being silly.
And then our romance with the sun
set as our backdrop,
and just the right mood to draw us in.

Long walks on the white sand with our bare feet,
Our hands intertwined and
content smiles on our faces.
Our emotions are reflections of serene
happiness and pure bliss.
For our paradise was with each other, and the
memories just for you and I.

But goods times are short.
So became our time together.
But this is just distance.
Nature brought us together and joy to our lives.
So we know neither distance
nor time can separate us.

Because against all odds,
we will be together.
For we are the only ones
who can relive our memories
and give each other paradise once again.

For now we still have the memories.
And any time I feel lonely for you,

I have the memories to comfort me,
until we share the same physical space once again.
And create more or our very own paradise.

LIFE

Seriously, we need to talk.
Talk about what?
About life, whatever this is…about us.

What about life? What about us?
It's not going like we planned.
Sweetie, then that's life.
Unpredictable, challenging, complex.
And then there's us.

What about us?
It's not going like we planned.
We are different, yet the same.
We love each other but do not
like each other all the time.
Yet we feel each other more than ever.
Life is not worth it without you.

Honey, that's life. That's us.
We can't control everything.
Let's just live life and enjoy each other.

What about love?
Yes, what about love?
That's life's gift to us. It's better than I thought,
and I am glad we found each other.

We can face life's ups and downs together.
You are the only part of life I am sure of.
And that's the best part of life.
It's working just fine for us.
Life gave us each other.

CURIOUS

I am a restless soul, a wanderer with a prying mind.
I can't sit still for long; I have to keep moving.
I have to stand up and see, it doesn't matter what.
I have to get up and go, it doesn't matter where.

My mind is curious, I have to keep inquiring.
My instinct tells me not to settle.
My instinct tells me to keep asking.
I trust my instinct, though it makes me restless.

There is more beyond now. Now is not enough.
There is more to know and more to see.
There are people to meet and more to seek.

The world is vast with boundless possibilities.
The people; extremely complex
and remarkably different.
I could learn a lot from them and
I could impact their lives as well.
Gee, there is so much to enjoy!

Yet I have so little time in the mist of the unlimited,
endless wonderment of this world.

It's no wonder why I am inquisitive.
It no wonder why I am a restless, curious being.
With my limited time and my colossal appreciation for
existing, I just need to know.

MOTHER

As a child, I always looked forward to
being with you.
When I cried on your shoulders,
you made things right.
When I hurt myself, I got a kiss and
a hug from you, and
the pain went away. When I was hungry,
I only wanted to
eat at home because you cooked the meals
with spices of love.

I love the fact that I can always count on you.
I love knowing that you'll
always be there for me.
I love knowing you'll be there to
mend my broken heart
and encourage me to keep my dreams alive.
I take comfort in knowing that
you want what's best for me
and that you pray for my safety each day.

When we fight, it breaks my heart.
But at the same time, we don't always
have to get along or say 'I love you,'
to know we really do care about each other.
You have always been and always be my mother
whose love can never ever be compared.

When I think of you as I often do,
I thank God for you, my mother,
and I really would have no one else.

There's a spot in my heart, which can never be
replaced by anyone because you,
my mother has that spot for life.

FACE OF THE MIND

I close my eyes, and I see your face.
It is as clear to me as night and day.
I've looked for you at various stages of my life,
and you have never once failed me.
You are my stranger, my friend, my sister,
and my mother all rolled into one.

In pain, I close my eyes, and search for your face.
You appear in a second, and comfort me.
In joy, I close my eyes and
search for your face again.
You appear in a second, and flash me
a proud, genuine smile.
In fun, I search for your face to share the excitement,
In an instance, you appear and we laugh together.
Then I know I'm doing okay.

Whether or not you exist, in my mind,
you are very real.
It is not my imagination.
I carry your image everywhere I go.
You are a part of my past, and
a part of my present existence.
I know without a doubt, you are going to be a part of
my future existence, because our
bonding goes far beyond
the natural human understanding.

You are the face of my mind.

SOULMATES

You may have been someone else in the past world
and I may have been someone else as well.
But somehow I believe we were soul mates then,
and I loved you with all I had to offer.
In this world, you are you and I am me
and I still love you with all I have got.

In the next world, I know we will still be soul mates.
and the two halves that makes us whole.
I know I will need you to be complete
and I hope you will feel the same way about me too.

For I believe that it was written in the stars
that we were meant to be. If there is a higher being,
I thank him for this one favor.
I knew I was lucky in the past world when
our two worlds came together.
I know for a second time that I am lucky now
as our two worlds merge again.

And now I hope I am lucky in the next world
and our two paths will cross again.
Somehow I don't doubt I will be lucky,
because I loved you even before I met you.

LONELY

In my heart burns a lonely soul,
crying silently for a little love,
and for someone to care about me.

I am hoping desperately for some kindness,
and wishing deeply that there be a sign,
that shows the reason for my existence,
and my place in the world.

Unwanted and unloved is all I have felt
for as long as I can remember.
Now I push away memories for most of
them are sad. But I never cease to hope
even very faintly, that the next morning begins
brightly as a sign of a better and happier future.

Though it may be for a short while,
at least I will have known my place in the world
and the reason why I am here.

For that short period in time,
I would have experienced
a little happiness and a sense of belonging.
For that period in time, my solitary
heart will be a happy heart.
And my being will be lonely no more.

ENCOUNTER

It was just another day at the beach in
a foreign country.
Happy sun-worshippers, swimmers
and beach-lovers alike
just enjoying a leisure day.
There were water rights, ice cream
and snack stands, photo seasons, music and dancing.
And then there was that one click,
that moment when
two strangers got together to take a
picture just for the hell of it.

Their eyes connected and for the rest of the day,
their magic was evident.
It was as though they had known each other forever.
They both knew the moment they took a picture
together on that faithful day
that it would be an encounter
that would change their future forever.
They met each other.

It was the beginning of a beautiful friendship.
And something more because then came love.
He told her he loved her and she smiled
coyly without responding.
But her heart beat a thousand times faster because
she was scared of her feelings for him.
How is it possible to feel this
strongly for another person?
So she waited for a while to be sure
it was just not a crush.

When he told her he loved her again,
this time she said it back.
Their encounter was a gift from the universe.
They were each other's gifts.
Their magic was obvious from the moment
they encountered each other and took a picture.

VISION OF A KNIGHT

She screamed in pain as she fell.
The blow to her head was hard as blood
gushed out like a running stream.
Her distorted expression and painful
scar hid a pretty face and once charming smile.
She couldn't move and her environment
was strange to her.
Then out of nowhere came her knight,
a simple stranger.
Not quite knowing what to do but seeing her
so broken in pain,
he lifted her up with his strong arms
and flagged down a cab
to the nearest hospital.

He was a stranger alone in a strange city.
So he came to the hospital each day
and sat by her bedside
as she drifted in and out of consciousness.
He was drawn to her for reasons he
could not fathom hoping she would get well soon,
willing her to wake up, willing her to get well.
Finally after a long while, she woke up to find him
by her bedside.

She could barely speak but he knew she was
going to be okay.
It was now time for him to leave.
It took her a few days but she came to understand

that he saved her life.
She never saw him again but forever imprinted in her
mind was her vision of a knight.

WATER

Water from my eyes, are tears of my pain,
and sadness in my heart.

Water from my face, is sweat from my burden,
and sign of my toil under the sun.

Water from above, is the source of my cleanliness,
and the reason I feel fresh everyday.

Water from the ground, quenches my thirst,
and is the reason I feel alive each day.

Water from my womb,
is evidence of my womanhood
because someone will exist through me.

Water from within, is sign of my labor,
and a sign someone will exist through me.

Water from the sea, is the source of my calmness,
and key to my peace.
In essence, water is the reason for my being.

TWO WORLDS

Going to sleep, I exit this world and walk right
in to my dreams.
I am fully alert and meet great people.
We go through exciting adventures together,
and life is nothing but a blast.
Life is perfect and there is not a care in the world.

Waking up I exit my dream world and
walk right back into the real world.
Too much clutter here.
Too much awareness of the disconnected minds.
I am fully aware of my surroundings.
I meet many people but we are nothing but strangers
all going through the motions of living day to day.

Sometimes if we are lucky if we get to
know one another
and maybe form a form a bond for life.
If we are lucky, that's it. Life is constantly changing.
Nothing is perfect. Everything is unexpected.
There are god days and there are bad days.
Two worlds of my person.
So very different yet so very much a part of me.

GEM

I just want to be with you forever.
Hurting you would be a crime.
You bring out the best in me.
Just being with you makes my day.

Your sweetness smoothens out my rough edges.
Your smile melts away my icy front.
The twinkle in your eyes were meant to be a
part of the stars in the sky.
Getting to know you each day is like an adventure
I don't want to end.
You make me feel like everyday
is a special occasion.

Just being yourself is what makes
you such a special person.
You are a trip I enjoy taking each day.
You have a heart of gold.
I struck out when I found you, my precious gem.

CRY

My heart is heavy with sadness.
Just like a heavy lid on a lightweight can.
My voice can sing no joy because
in my heart there is pain.
I cry out for help for someone to release me
from this torture.
But it seems that I am trapped in
a room with no exit,
and walls made of solid brick.

There seem to be no chance of escape.
I cannot get out. I can only move in circles.
I try once again like I have done many times before,
to pave an opening through the wall but
once again it is fruitless.

I am tired anyway, for my strength is dwindling.
It is hard for me to breathe because
there is no fresh air.
My thirst is strong and my voice cracks but there is no
water to quench my thirst.

My stomach grumbles with hunger,
but there is no food in sight.
My cries are tearless because
there are no more tears to be shed from me.
I have exhausted myself.

With what's left of my voice,
I make another tearless cry.
Someone please listen to me!
Someone please hear me!

Someone please say a prayer for me
as I become voiceless
with sadness and alone in this invisible darkness.

All I ask is enough saving grace to give me
the hope and courage I need to go on in life.

SUBSTANCE

You are what makes me.
You give substance to my person.
My passion and my pleasure is you.
You are the outlet to my freedom of expression.
This comes from the bottom of my heart.
You give me the courage to be myself.

You keep me going each day by breathing
life into me in the form of your generous love,
and selfless attitude.
You are like a rare treasure I feel I don't deserve.

My life is completely bright because you
put a smile each day on my heart each day.
You are the comforter of my sorrow when
I feel misunderstood and lonely.
You dry the tears on my face when I'm sad.
You are the glue that puts back
broken pieces of my life.

I can accept the person that I am because
you accept me without question
and without condition.
You are my daily source of inspiration,
You are my hope for a better tomorrow.
You are my best friend, and my true love,
you are simply the whole of me.

BELIEVER

I believe in me.
Sometimes I doubt myself but most of the times,
I believe in me.
No one would give me a chance to show
what a great person I am but I still believe in me,
because I know me best.

I know in my heart, I am capable of bigger
and better things. I know with my brain,
I am capable of the smartest things.
I know with my hands,
I can create the most wonderful things,
because I believe in me without a doubt.

And they can all be damned
because one way or another,
I'll give me a chance and disappoint those
who doubt me. I know I am good.
Hell, I believe I am or can be the best because I
believe in me.

MOTHER AND CHILD

My greatest joy was bringing you into this world.
It was the most joyful pain I ever experienced.
When I held your tiny form in my arms
and looked at your little face,
I could not help but feel a sense of wholeness.
I am now bonded for life to another human being.

And then you let out the biggest wail
your little voice could take.
Immediately I felt an overwhelming sense of
protection and love for you.
And I promised myself that
I would try to protect you from any
harm the world might bring
because you are a part of me.
The moment you were conceived,
we became the same.
In two physical forms but extension of each other.

My joy each day is just watching you grow.
Every breath you take and every sound you make,
makes my heart beat with pride and joy.
I cannot help but wonder everyday
at the miracle of birth,
and the power I have been given by God
to be able to create life.
I am now responsible for a living being like myself.

My child, you and I have will intertwined
for the rest of our lives.
But alas, I also worry each day as you grow older.

My fear is watching you get sick
and being helpless about it.
I worry about you not coming back home each day.
I am filled with anxiety when I can't protect you from
the harsh realities of life.
I feel every pain, and every joy, and every
accomplishment you make in life.
Our lives are forever intertwined.

But no matter what is in store for you or for me,
I wouldn't trade motherhood
for anything in the world.
I feel completely whole.
I am a woman. I am a mother.
I was born to nurture.
I accomplish something special each day
of my life as I think of you, my child.
I am a mother for life.

Now I know that even though we as women,
carry a lot of life's burdens,
At the very beginning, God made it up to us
by giving us the power to create
life and be called mothers for the rest of our lives.
You are my child. I am your mother.

We are each other's miracles.
We are intertwined for life.
We are one. We are miracles of life.
We celebrate the same birthday;
the day I gave birth to you and
the day that you were born.
We are bonded for life.
We are mother and child.

THE OTHER SIDE

Somewhere behind this facade lies me. The real me.
The me that feels and the me that hurts.
Broken, wounded, and lonely me.
The me that only I understand and no one else does.
The me that no one else cares about,
and the me that even I,
sometimes think does not deserve anyone's care.

Somewhere behind this exterior lies me.
The real me.
The me that is sad and the me that feels hopeless.
Restless, discouraged and unlucky me.
The me that pretends not to care and
the me that even I sometimes
think does not deserve to have
the good things in life.

Somewhere behind this persona lies me.
The real me.
The me that has very little confidence,
and the me that is unsure.
Shy, discouraged and scared me.
The me that pretends to be bold and the me that
sometimes even
I do not think has any reason to be proud.

Somewhere behind this act lies me.
The real me.
The me that is fed up and the me that is tired.
Worn out, hopeless and exhausted me.
The me that acts tough and the me that
acts as though my shoulders

are wide enough to carry all the burdens of
life without any support.

On the other side of the mirror stands me.
The real me.
The me that is tired of working so damn hard,
when rewards are not forthcoming.
The me, as only I understand, that is so damn tired of
being on life's battle filed.
The me that is so damn tired of
being unfortunate and unlucky.

Well this me, is just about ready to give up.
Because for me, as only I understand,
sees no reason to hope.
For the eyes of me, sees the real me
standing on the other side.
The eyes of me see no light at the
end of the dark tunnel.

CLASS ACT

She was not beautiful by society's standards.
She was short, overweight and had dark skin.
Her clothes were old and mismatched.
She did not have much to call her own.
She lived in a poor section of town.

Yet by higher standards, she was a class act.
She exuded confidence and inner beauty,
which surpassed any physical attribute.

Adults and children gravitated
towards her all the time.
Even the cool teenagers would rather be around her.
She made any place feel alive
and everyone feel special.
She was the one everyone aspired to be like.
You see, she had that inner beauty,
which everyone wished they had but only few had.

Though she was poor, and her house was small,
she welcomed everyone into her house.
Because it was not a house but a
home filled with laughter,
love and the smell of a sweet home-cooked meal..
Her food was not gourmet but it was much richer
and tastier with spices made of love.

She had everything everyone wanted.
She was a class act.

IT

It's not the type of house that you live in.
Nor the type of car that you drive.
It's not the job that you have,
nor the title that you hold.
It's not how much money that you make.
Neither is it the clothes that you wear, nor the shoes,
nor the jewelry.
It is not how well traveled you are,
Nor is it how much education you have that matter.

Rather, it is the poetry in you.
It is the heart that you have.
It is the manner of your expression.
It is what makes up your person.
That's what defines you.
That's what captured me.
It is the essence of you.

FATHER AND SON

My son, you are God's gift to me.
I am overcome with joy and love when I look at you.
I now have an overwhelming
responsibility toward you for life.
But I take pride in the fact that
you are now a grown man.
You are what makes me a real man.

Just as I have a responsibility
toward your mother and siblings,
you too will carry the same responsibility
as a fully-grown man.
We as men are supposed to be relied on
completely in times of crisis.
We are taught as men to defend ourselves and ours.
We are taught to treat women with respect because
they brought us to this world to be men.

You are now a grown man.
Though you and I are not big on words,
we understand
each other because we are men.
Sometimes, we bury our emotions beneath our pride
but between you and I,
we understand our silent gestures.
We read each other's eyes and
we understand our thoughts.
We are men.

Just as I will always be a son to my father,
you will always be a son to me.
We will bear the same name for life.

It is our job to carry that name with pride.
We will think and look like each
other till our time on earth is over.

You are my single greatest pride in life.
I now live through you. We are bonded for life.
We are father and son.

ME, MYSELF AND I

We were all born together, me, myself and I.
We grew up feeling a bit odd.
We always felt like the black sheep in the family.
Always misunderstood, never quite noticed.

We always had to try extra hard to get
what others got normally.
In fact, if the truth be said,
we still feel like that on many occasions.
But that's just us, hoping to belong.
This is who we are, me, myself and I.

At the risk of blowing our own horns,
I should say on behalf of my other two selves;
we are actually very pleasant or so we have been told
on a number of occasions by many people.
But that's the plus side.

On the minus side, we have been taken advantage
off so many times that I have lost count.
So we decided to stand up for our selves.
Enough already!
After all, me, myself and I stand for something.
But at the end of the day,
we are still just a work in progress,
trekking through life's challenges like everyone else.

Me, myself and I, a work in progress.
An unfinished business.

TODAY

Today, I'm going to take time to smell the roses.
I'm going to take a walk in the park,
and breathe in the fresh air.

Today, I'm going to smile and
push away my worries.
I'm going to waive to strangers and
push away my worries.
I'm going to wave to strangers and laugh
in a carefree manner.

Today, I'm going to take one step at a time,
and enjoy each moment.
I'm going to be simple unknown me.
Just one of many strangers.

Today, I'm just going to enjoy living
before life passes me by.
Today is my day.
Today is my gift.

MEANING OF LOVE

Someone asked me to explain the meaning of love.
I immediately said your name.
He said no, that's not what he meant.
He wanted me to define love,
and I said your name again.
He looked puzzled and I couldn't understand why.
Because very simply, you are the definition of love.
I know without a doubt I think of you
when I think of love.

I feel whole with you in my life.
I feel loved and appreciated just for being me.
I don't feel the need to hide behind a façade,
or pretend to be someone I am not.
I don't feel alone in a strange environment.
I am not afraid to face the world because I have you in
my corner. I have love.

I see you inner beauty and your beautiful heart.
My face lights up in a content smile
when I think of you.
I am happy and at peace because
I have you in my life.
I have love. I see love when I see you.
I understand love when I speak to you.
I know without a doubt the definition of love.
Love is you.

DRIFTER

I came to this world alone.
It is a vast world and there are plenty of people.
But I don't know anyone
because I am a lonely drifter.

I am a stranger to people and likewise,
they are to me.
I am just passing by but I know that
I will stop when I get home.
I don't know where home is but I'll know
when I get there.
For now, I am a lonely drifter.

I am still on my way.
I may be sailing on my own and I may be a stranger,
but I have been touched by
life's trials and tribulations,
and people's experiences, along the way.
For this reason, I am passing by this world;
to learn life's lessons and to learn
how to calm the storms of life.

When my mission is complete and
I have touched people lives
by my own experiences as they have
touched mine likewise,
I will drift away on my own lonely sail.

I will finally know I am sailing on the
right direction toward home.

IYE

She was feisty. She was funny. She was sweet.
She was my Iye.
And yes, she spoke her mind.
She was ever so protective of hers.
Hers being her children
and hers being her grandchildren.
She also loved fiercely and yes
she was loved right back.
How I loved her. How I will miss her.
She was my Iye. She was my Grandma.

I remember her. I remember her love.
She was my Granny.
I remember how happy I felt when I was in the
company of my Iye.
And yes, I recall the joy I felt as a child every evening
when she was came home from the market carrying
products on her head.
Our first instincts as grandkids were to run toward her
screaming "Iye dede oyoyo!"
Our grandmother has come back.
We knew what to expect.
My Iye always had a treat ready for each
of her grandchildren.

I also recall my grandmother saying
"Ayo must eat" when she was sharing food for us.
That's my Iye for sure.
My loving feisty granny.
Her love was safe, her love was nurturing.
Her love meant never being hungry.
And I can say with absolute certainty

that her food was tasty because she cooked
with spices of love.

Iye was also radiant.
Elegant and well dressed even at her age.
The last time I saw her, I was just so happy.
I felt her love so deeply and at that moment
all was well with the world.
I was with my Grandma.
She was my Iye.
Her loyalty to hers was total.
Her love was total. She was my Iye.

My grandma, my Iye.
Never forgotten, always remembered
with so much love.

ME

I am me.
Through the years I have grown older with age
and wiser with time.
I have gone through various changes in life,
and I have matured with age.
But I am still me.

I have gone through all of life's emotions.
I have been sad, and I have been happy.
I have been made softer by life's circumstances.
And I have been made tougher as well.
But deep down I am me. I simply feel like me.

On occasions, I put up a front and pretend to
be someone I am not. But behind that pretense,
and inside that strange person taking over my
body and my voice, I exist.

When things calm down, and I am strong again,
I take back my personality and my being.
And me, the person that I am, and the person that
I have always known, comes out again as
it always does.

Because me, the person that I am,
has already been created to exist and
made to form since the day that I was born.

THE INNOCENT

Beautiful when they are born.
Of pure hearts and minds.
Joyous to all around them.
Giving unconditional love with a wail,
a yawn and a smile.
Our children, our innocents.

Seeing the world in black and white.
Nothing is green, gray or in-between.
All they understand is 'I want, I need.'
It is the world is according to them.
If only they knew but they don't.

They are special. To them the world is simple.
Nothing is complicated. They are our children.
They are the innocents.

MY SOMEONE

Who are you and what is your name?
In the nighttime when I go to sleep,
you invade my dreams.
In the daytime as I go about my life,
you invade my thoughts.
I cannot see your eyes because you hide
them behind dark glasses.
I can only see part of your hair because you always
have a baseball cap on.

Each time I close my eyes,
I see you coming toward me,
gliding on those roller blades and
a sure smile on your face.
And still you wear those cream-colored
pair of shorts and a white T-shirt.
I have now come to know you only
so well in my dreams.

I wonder if you are real?
Or am I just imagining you?
Sometimes when I close my eyes,
I could almost touch you.
Are you a friend, enemy or lover?
I feel your lingering presence everywhere I go.
Or maybe you are really my guardian angel?

Now I search for you everywhere.
Without a doubt, I am sure I will know you the
moment I see you.

Because even though we have never actually met,

I feel as though I already know you.
For some reason you have become a part of my life.
And since I don't know your name,
I will simply call you My Someone
because in the mist of my dreams,
we have already met.

EN ROUTE

To some, there is hope, to others, hopelessness.
To some, there is faith,
to others, doubt.
To some, there is happiness,
to others, sadness.
To some, there is confidence, to others, shyness.

A little hope and a little faith
can bring us closer to our dreams.
A little encouragement and a little boldness should
make us think it is worth a fight.

But simple as this sounds,
it takes a little miracle, just enough courage,
and a step bold enough to take the risky
route to living our truth.

FOR PEACE SAKE

For peace sake, let me be your friend
and care about you.
You can tell me to back down but
for peace sake, don't ask me to back off.
Because I'll always be behind you,
regardless of what you do.

You can tell me to shut up but for peace sake
don't mean it forever.
Because, I'll always give you advise
whenever you need it.

You can tell me to leave you alone
but for peace sake,
don't forget that you are never alone
whenever you are sad.
Because I'll be right there in the wings
with my arms wide open
just waiting to comfort you.

You can tell me to disappear from your life
but for peace sake, don't erase me from your mind.
Because I'll never stop thinking about you.
You can tell me I'm no longer important to you
but for peace sake, don't ask me to stop loving you.
Because that's just something
I would never be able to do.

Like the night turning into daylight and the stars
beautifying the night, loving you is just as natural,
and caring for you is like a second nature.

So for peace sake, just let me be
and care about you forever.

IN TRUTH

In truth, we are for real.
Don't apologize and don't explain,
because I understand.
That's why we are connected.

In truth, we are for real.
Don't worry and don't be anxious because
we are in this together.
That's why we have each other.

In truth, we are for real.
Don't cry and don't be unhappy
because we can pick up the pieces together.
That's why we are friends.

In truth, we are for real.
Don't be scared to express your hopes
and go after yours dreams because
I'll be right there to nudge
you along the way.
That's why we care about each other.

In truth, we are for real.
To laugh with each other and to cry with each other,
to help each other overcome obstacles
as we make our way through life because in truth,
we are for always.
In truth we are for real.

LIVING EACH DAY

We live a piece of our future each day.
In wisdom, we find the strength we need
to deal with life's challenges each day in a manner
that will aid our peace of mind.

In faith, we find the courage and patience
we need to overcome obstacles in our paths.

We hope for happiness and we hope for peace.
We hope for courage and we hope for strength.
But most of all, we simply hope that
we are fortunate enough to live
to see the next day and to live our lives
to the fullest each day.

CELEBRATION

Love is a celebration of life.
The highest gift that can ever be blessed with.
The greatest power of all.
It can never be bought.

Some people are lucky to be born into love,
and some are lucky to be born with love.
Some have the gift to be able to give love
and others will do anything to get love.

Love can never be bought with money.
It is simply something to be thankful about.
People who have it should treasure it.
Those who yearn for it should not give up.
Because love's rays are very long.
It can reach the most isolated person in the world.
It is a universal language.

It is understood and wanted by everyone.
Wish for it if you want it. Celebrate it if you have it.
Treasure it because it is power.
Because love is a celebration of life.

SUNSHINE

You are as bright as the sun that lights up
my world each day.
It may be snowing and it maybe raining for all I care,
but in my world, there is sunshine.
I wake up each morning and you are the first person
I look at as you lie down beside me.
Immediately, a sunny smile forms on my face
because I know it is going to be a pleasant day.
I have you in my life.

You are the sunshine of my life.
For this, I am grateful for each day.
It may be cloudy and it may be dark for all I care
but in my world, it is a sunny day.
I go to bed each night and you are the last person
I see as you lay down beside me.
Immediately, a feeling of contentment
washes over my being.
Because, I know once again that I am
going to bed with the
love of my life and a sunny heart of happiness.

I look forward to living everyday because
I spend each day with you.
In my world there is no sadness
and there is no darkness.
There is only joy because you are the sunshine
that makes my life worth living.
You are the sunshine of my world.

Just so you know...

Also by Irene Ayo Asuen

Not Quite Imperfect (novel, just released)
Destiny's Faces (novel)
Destiny's Love (lyric poem)
Destiny's Anguish (lyric poem)
Just My Opinion, But … (coming soon)

Also available in bookstores, retail outlets and other sites including Barnes and Noble, Lulu, iBooks, Play.Google, Kobo, Overdrive, Smashwords and others.

Also available in eBook format.

NOT QUITE IMPERFECT

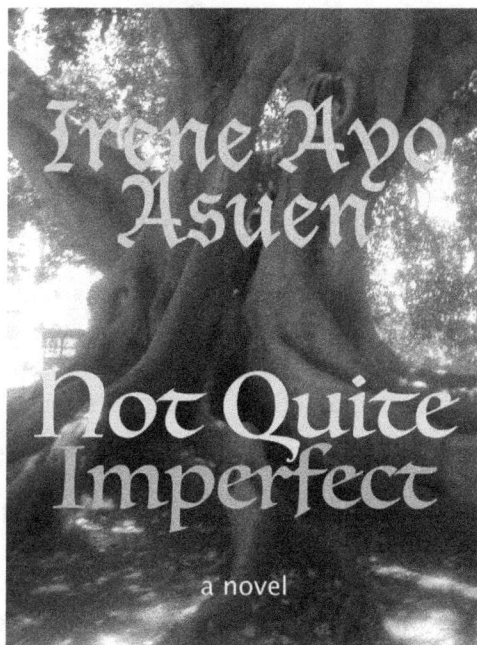

Irene Ayo Asuen

Not Quite Imperfect

a novel

Not Quite Imperfect is a character-driven, drama-filled story that explores human connection, tragedy, betrayal, survival and redemption.

At age 35, Ian Sharp, a tall, handsome, African-American man with lean athletic features, was well aware of his good looks and irresistible charisma because he usually counted on them to get him out of life's sticky binds. More importantly, these attributes were his gifts to women. That is, until he met Kendra

Mercury, and everything became, well, complicated. From the moment that Ian spotted Kendra as she was crossing the street on Sunset Boulevard in Los Angeles, he had chased her relentlessly until she agreed to be his. But their relationship was not that simple. Kendra tested him. She challenged him, she drove him crazy, she loved him, she confused him, she tolerated him and damn, she was quite the stubborn woman. Ian Sharp was not used to this...

Kendra Mercury, 33, was a slender, beautiful, African-American woman of average height; slightly flared nose and a crooked smile that revealed a slight gap between her two top teeth. Kendra had the right outlook to life and an engaging personality. By anyone's standards, she was the total package. Men constantly made passes at her but it was Ian that made her heart soar. After Kendra met Ian, the "smart, logical" Kendra that friends and family had always known, had morphed into, well, someone else. But the way Kendra saw it, *"no one knew Ian like she did..."*

Ian and Kendra were magical together but their relationship was more than a tad complicated. You see, Ian never pretended to want children, and because Kendra loved Ian, she pushed aside her own desire to be a mom for years...until Liana happened, and Kendra could no longer deny her own desires. Of course Ian was pissed and demanded that Kendra make a decision. Kendra did, and walked away from him.

Unfortunately, without Kendra, Ian's world had not been not 'normal' since they broke up. So after seven years apart, and unable to get her out of his head, Ian bulldozed his way back to Kendra's life in the worst possible way: blackmail. But by the time Ian resurfaced into Kendra's life, Peter Rite had already become a huge part of her world, because two years after breaking up with Ian, while minding her business in a midtown Manhattan café, Peter Rite happened ...

Peter, a book cover designer from Brooklyn, was six years Kendra's junior, five feet, ten inches tall, and handsome. Yep, Peter was definitely easy on the eyes. When he spotted Kendra in the café, he just knew she was the face of his heart...

There was no denying that Peter and Kendra had quite the effect on each other or that Kendra and Ian were each other's drug of choice despite their years apart and complicated history. While Peter exuded quiet confidence and authority, Ian's presence and charisma could almost be touched. It led to one big complicated mess. And of course, there was still the matter of Liana…

Rejected by the man that gave her life but accepted by another that loved her like his flesh and blood, Liana was in the middle of the triangle that was Kendra, Ian and Peter for different reasons. However, all their issues took a turn one day when life threw everyone a curveball as Peter's destiny is decided, Kendra looses the will to live, Liana's ability to ever live a healthy, normal life again hangs in a balance, Ian finds himself in a unique position of having to make a life-changing decision that could finally connect him to the daughter that he once wished was never born, and everyone else in-between, is left reeling from the effect of the whole situation…

There is more to the story…

Not Quite Imperfect is a new novel by Irene Ayo Asuen that has just been published.

www.ireneayoasuen.com

"Open your mind and explore the possibilities…"

QuietlySpeaking™